ALSO BORN OF THE FIRE

Poetry by Patricia Ryan

Outskirts Press, Inc.
Denver, Colorado

Outskirts Press, Inc.
http://www.outskirtspress.com

ISBN: 978-1-4327-2751-2

Outskirts Press and the "OP" logo are trademarks belonging to Outskirts Press, Inc.

PRINTED IN THE UNITED STATES OF AMERICA

FOREWORD

Also Born of the Fire is the first published collection of Patricia Ryan's poetry. After more than forty years of honing her craft, having studied with San Francisco Bay Area poets at San Francisco State, such as Frances Mayes, Kathleen Fraser, William Dickey, and Jack Marshall, and more recently, leading writing workshops and a poetry writing group for ten years, "Read and Write Like a Woman," this poet gifts her readers with this astounding and perceptive body of poetry that in turn, stuns, delights, challenges, and questions her readers.

Like all poets, Patricia writes from within her unique life-world, the context from within which her poetic voice and consciousness emerge. It is not the usual combination of influences. She is a native of the San Francisco Bay Area, with family roots in the Pacific Northwest and a deep love for her Irish heritage. Her poetry evokes, re-presents, closely observes and reflects on these particular bioregions. These are the landscapes we meet in her poems. In college she was a chemistry major and an English minor, as well as a violinist. A Roman Catholic Sister of Mercy for more than fifty years, she taught math, science, religion, and fine arts appreciation in secondary schools for many years. Influenced by Zen as well as by Christianity, she is also an ecologist, social justice activist, and a feminist. Poems may draw on one, two, three or four of these life-world confluences, layering and exploding in image and meaning within a single poem. Across, this corpus, the perceptive reader witnesses and senses a constantly evolving consciousness becoming more and more original, cosmological, non-stereo-typically religious and feminist regardless of the announced subject matter of a particular poem.

Poems within the collection are grouped under six themes around fire, sun, questions, patriotism, feminism, and religion. These categories are capacious and also suggestive since many poems could be read within more than one general category.

The title poem, *The Flower-also born of the fire* juxtaposed as it is with a line from T.S. Eliot, "The fire and the rose are one," holds in tension the fragile beauty of flowers and the fierce originating fire of the universe. This is the first of many poems focused on origins, the beginnings, creation. Transposed into the key of the new cosmology, beauty/love and solar energy are held together. The association of rose, daffodils and tulips as having "endured the furnace," being "another sunrise," or "burning" in a field compel the reader to embrace the primacy of fire—the fire-ball of the origin of all that is, the delicate beauty of every bloom, no less than ourselves. In this poem, the presence of Divinity is barely alluded to, implied in the lines,

> Fire awakened first
> called to fill the emptiness
> with a unifying
> YES.

Who or what calls is left unnamed. Subsequent poems make Creator God more explicit but certainly not more comfortable.

> In the beginning
> God preceded beginning

> In the beginning- fire
> Before the beginning-nothing

> The sight of the fire burning nothing
> Raises the great prayer- Aha.

Affirmation is followed by negation. Religious awe rises from the mystery of the fire burning nothing. A similar sense of awe is engendered in *Fear* through the symbol of Mount Sinai as a physical location on the same planet as ourselves and the poet's image of "angels perspiring fire from fear of the Holy."

Just as the double-edged mystery of fire blazes through the poems in this section, so too, do the poignancy and fragility of flowers. Meditative consciousness

> looks and sees
> the slowly blooming rose

> live as the flower
> and equally aware
> of its own interaction
> with surrounding air.

In *Roots*, ecological indifference and environmental pollution is ascribed to the insight "we have no roots in the earth." The poet embraces with great compassion the gesture of a floating memorial wreath of white flowers, placed in a canal even though the wreath is as equally polluting as beer cans and cardboard cartons. Yet the closing image stuns us with its fragile beauty.

> The flowers had no roots in the wreath.
> Bound to die, yet dazzling
> For a time.

The second section of the collection is filled with sunrises, sunsets, and waiting for the light. The tone moves from playful whimsy, to tenderness, to sheer terror.

> What if
> the sun never set
> but just sat out there
> laughing
> at the ashes?

The poems encompass the memory of a soggy camping trip with teen-age girls waiting for the light in extreme discomfort, to multiple shifts of perspective in a poem subtly playing on the religious theme of conversion-- turning around, seeing something differently, from "facing, to turning, to waiting." In a sense, every poem invites the reader to a change in *Perspective*, not just the one that ponders whether west is on your left or right? It is the poet's craft to so use language that we cannot continue to see things the same old way. *Homelessness* coaxes the reader to identify with the condition of homelessness, not something most of us are wont to do.

> So we all are
> with few exceptions on the streets
> pavement of our own making
> far from the caves of ancestors
> who lived in the earth.

As this poem unfolds, the sacred liminal spaces of living within earth are contrasted with the "outside"—disease, sickness, death, hollowness. And the movement of the poem secures our assent to a new beatitude,

> Blessed, those who know
> they are homeless
> who stand in the rain
> with soaked shopping carts
> intent on the horizon
> warmed at the fireside
> of the great sinking sun.

It is this capacity to seduce the reader into the world of the poem and into an entirely new awareness of our common human condition that occurs over and over again in the subsequent sections that invite us to live with the unanswerable questions of life as well as our painful betrayal of our country's deepest values in waging unjust and self-destructive wars, *Current Exegesis,* our rejection of refugees, *Like Seed,* and our basic lack of awareness, *Awakening.*

This latter poem is so multivalent that it could apply to many, many different situations of failing to heed the warnings. The poem's situation places the reader squarely on the Titanic, pondering not listening, not believing the warnings, keeping reality at bay, yet the "unwanted awareness" arrives anyway through the sparse lines of the poem.

> Now what to do
> this unwanted awareness
> of menacing water
> beyond the flimsy hatches.

Among my personal favorites in this collection is *Violin*. It is a poignant narrative of the poet's relationship with her violin, her own musical talent. While it expresses ambivalence about her musical gifts personified in the violin she addresses throughout the poem, she also captures the utter power of music played with technical skill and such a fullness of feeling that it can transform the most unlikely person. One senses the depths of the poet's musical sensibility both as listener and performer.

Tsunami addresses survivors of the event in Southeast Asia, some of whom were relatives of the poet. After two verses describing the tidal wave and those it claimed, the poem asks two questions of the survivors-- questions anyone of us who is still alive might well ponder.

> Do you often reflect
> on what it is
> that you still have to do?

> Are you trying
> Not to waste
> This precious time
> That you still have to become you?

These are provocative poems, prodding us into deeper awareness of our taken-for-granted lives.

The fifth section invites the reader into an explicitly feminist consciousness wrestling with women's subjugation, including the colonization of women's minds. Some of these poems are playful, others ironic, subversive, startling, angry, pained. The poems themselves demonstrate how difficult it is for women to write and think like a woman. The language itself has to be wrested away from masculine domination and hierarchy, tamed and reclaimed-- the myths revised, mined for fresh hints of possibility.

In *Garden*, the poet plunges us into an alternative story of the Garden of Eden. She describes the patterns of thinking that confuse the woman who is never named. We discover the fear at woman's core and how she uses it. Finally, the questions in the last two verses open entirely fresh ways of thinking, feeling, and behaving.

> Why did you leave the garden?
> It is his god
> driving him
> from the garden
> Why do you go?
>
> Among the things
> which he builds
> out of extra ribs
> you
> are near the top
> Is that why you leave?
> Are you climbing
> the tree
> instead of eating
> the apple?
>
> Why are you afraid of the apple?

The final section of poems grouped under the heading of religion's work of permanent astonishment does, indeed, astonish. Throughout the volume, the reader has already encountered many implicitly and explicitly religious themes and metaphors woven into other poems. Here they are more often explicit, evocative of the mystical intuition that can receive the full force of the challenge to meet God in a new and startling way. Doubt mingles with profound faith that does not need to make excuses for God. The poems probe the mystery of God's tenderness and otherness with great sensitivity. For example, *It is You* confronts the problem of natural disasters and God's love without resolving the struggle—only staying in the relationship stuns the questioner into incomprehension, leaving the mystery intact. *Beloved* plays with the paradox of beauty and power, and hints at the complexity of an intimate relationship with God that can reclaim bridal language after an earlier rejection. And *Incarnation* throbs with mystical intuition as the poet reflects on the cosmology in relationship to the theological symbol of incarnation. Is not the entire cosmos, God's body? Is not the entire world infused with divinity, not only the Virgin alone?

More than nine months
this infusion of divinity

What else
could have powered the explosion

And driven
this outward expansion

The living center
in infinite directions
becoming everywhere.

Is not this collection of poetry a form of Incarnation? I suspect it is, and invite you to taste these words for yourself, welcoming their potential to change your perspective and illuminate your own experience more deeply.

Dr. Janet Ruffing, RSM
Professor in Spirituality and Spiritual Direction
Fordham University
Bronx, New York

TABLE OF CONTENTS

ACKNOWLEDGEMENTS

In addition to gratitude to my family, and community for their loving presence on my life's journey, I am indebted to Sisters Genemarie Beegan and Janet Ruffing for their assistance and encouragement in bringing this book of poems to completion. I also want to acknowledge the valuable input of my monthly poetry writing group.

"The fire and the rose are one."

T. S. Eliot

THE FLOWER - also born of the fire   2004

The grandparents of each flower
soil   water   air

Yet every bloom
finds its roots in fire

The crimson petals of a rose
its delicate softness
have endured the furnace

Each emerging daffodil
is another sunrise

Near Anacortes, Washington
fields of tulips are burning

Fire awakened first
called to fill the emptiness
with a unifying
YES

IN THE BEGINNING 2006

In the beginning
God preceded beginning

In the beginning - fire
Before the beginning - nothing

The sight of fire burning nothing
Raises the great prayer - Aha

TWO FROM NINE GATES   *2005*

"...free from the distractions
of interest or boredom"

a mind that usually
cannot pass a puzzle
locked unswervingly
on the here and now

looks and sees
the slowly blooming rose

alive as the flower
and equally aware
of it's own interaction
with surrounding air

knowing that I cannot keep it
cannot keep anything

all is passing
at the instant
when all is here
and all is new

FLOWER(s) 2006

I

Why would you want to be
a single rose in a lovely vase
when you could be
a field of tulips
or a hill of daffodils

II

An open rose
its potential bared
realized

Its whiteness
in the captured fire
of all colors

Each petal
experiences wholeness

Any plastic image
fails in fragrance
in fragility

FER

2006

To think
of being on the same planet
as Mount Sinai
for so long
and never
having seen the angels
perspiring fire
from fear of the Holy

COMMISSION 1997

To the old trees
leave
the love songs

Blossoms
flee
the rugged wind

Amorphous embers
form
in the arms of fire

THE TREE'S ONLY JOURNEY IS UPWARDS
2003

If a tree needs to lean
its neighbors will support it

Swaying is undetectable
at the base of a trunk
non-existent underground
where roots are grasped by gravity

When passing clouds
see the stationary trees
they sometimes weep
knowing they will never find a home

But a tree takes these tears
turns them into bark
and leaves that often stay

EZEKIEL'S EASTER

Under the transparent score
lay a white egg
on a large flesh hand.
I heard a new heart
beating within the egg.
Silently it grew great sinews
and the flesh hand closed over it.
The notes sang Alleluia.

Centered in a tight field
of white flowers
was a single space.
A hand reached down
setting therein
a jasmine blossom, wet.
I was told that these white bones
had had death drained from them.

ROOTS

The problem is
we have no roots in the earth,
none of the grasses tenacity.
The wind could sweep us into the canal
where the evergreen wreath floats
amid the litter.

Most of the white flowers
had fallen from the wreath.
There were eleven left.
I searched it twice for twelve.

We, who lovingly placed our wreath
on waters, are one with those
tossing in the beer cans
and the cardboard cartons.
They too,
have no roots in the earth.

The flowers had no roots in the wreath.
Bound to die, yet dazzling
for a time.

When evolution is mentioned
some immediately jump
to ape
"Are you saying
my ancestors are apes?"

NO NO NO
our ancestors are
water   air   earth
and FIRE

NO NO NO
our ancestors are
protons, electrons, neutrons

NO NO NO
they're subatomic particles

NO
for years they had
only counting numbers
and then an Arab
imagined zero;

*"Our sun set in the sky
way before this earth was born,
waiting to caress a billion faces."*

Hafiz

THE STARS

1958

Listen to the stars
throbbing out their lives
with a heat that shouts
to all the universe
a tale of ageless intensity
which laughs at youthful planets
strutting in their new found being
and yanks them along
with a cry of streaking light
racing to the outer bounds
where they may turn and fall
and suddenly be stilled
in awe before their judge.

TERROR

1997

What if
the sun didn't come up
slow and easy;
if it startled us
like those nuisance lights

What if
the day couldn't be expected
and night went on
for years

And what if
the sun never set
but just sat out there
laughing
at the ashes

LATE FOR THE SUNSET   *1958*

Must you take the footlights
when you leave the stage?
We're left with nothing
but the remnant red
veil of the great hot-head
that just bowed out.

How I'd love to reach out
and grab you by the nape
and yank you back
to repeat the exit
and delay the Chinese entrance
so you'll know what it's like to be late!

DAILY
1997

Each morning we wake the sun
and hurry it on its way to work
For hours we expect it won't need us
until evening when we lay it to rest
in the cavernous west

EMERGENCE

2007

Watching
brilliant red, pink, orange
streaks across the morning sky
gradually fade into grey

when the long awaited
yellow ball casts its reflection
on the surface of the bay
and turns the clouds
pure white

BAT 1997

This morning
sitting quietly
in my meditation chair
I saw a bat
zipping across the sky.
In spite of past terror
I knew
that we were both
waiting for the sun.

LIGHT UPON LIGHT

The silver crescent sliver
moves so slowly
over the blackened treetops

Even though
it is surrounded by blinding light
its reflection is fingernail fine

What a lesson
to watch the cold dark surface
returning more light than it receives
to the Beloved

This faithful teacher
who points, points, points
then disappears

SUNSET 2007

Directly to our left
we sneaked glances

A band of clouds
artfully bent sunlight
in a brilliant performance
of rays and changing colors
on the ocean's ample stage

If an artist
had captured it on canvas
it would be judged artificial
not even close to probable

But there it was
with no admission charge

Regretfully we turned away
without having stopped
to look, much less listen

PERSPECTIVE

2002

(on conversion)

Is the west
On your left or your right?

It depends on
If you're facing north or south
(or to say it another way)
On if you're facing earth or sky

Facing seems to be the key
The why is because your eye
(round like the earth)
Can only look one way
Unless you turn

No, actually
You don't have to turn
The earth is turning for you

You only have to be
Willing to wait

The west is always coming toward you
Watch, it passes every evening
As the sun pulls down the sky

WAITLESS

2006

Waiting for the sun,
dipping into the deep well
of my impatience

The artist, irritated
by the scientist
who wanted to know
the exact point
on the hill tops
where it would creep over

The artist cried -
watch the colors
the gray clouds
turn pink, then red
and on to gold, then white
until the yellow
ball of fire
forces you to turn
your eyes away

HOMELESSNESS

So we all are
with few exceptions
on the streets
pavement of our own making
far from the caves of ancestors
who lived in the earth

The caves now are uninhabited
like gaps between mountains
space – sacred, nurturing,
liminal, between places
where emptiness is fullness
motion irrelevant

Outside
disease is contracted
sickness of prefabrication
sickness of speed
terminal creatures
heart hollow
who have moved often
but not deep into the caves

Blessed, those who know
they are homeless
who stand in the rain
with soaked shopping carts
intent on the horizon
warmed at the fireside
of the great sinking sun

DID YOU EVER

2008

spend a night
waiting for light?
We did

And were you lying in a tent
with another teacher and two teenagers?
We were

Were their feet
near your face?
They were

Had they crawled in for shelter
from the rainstorm outside?
They had

Were eight other kids
squeezed into the car?
They were

Did they keep opening and closing the door
so they could breathe?
They did

Was another teacher with other kids
standing in the restroom, shivering and wet?
She was

When morning rescued you, did you hike back out
with extremely heavy sleeping bags?
We did

Was the parking lot filled
with worried parents?
It was

Is this one reason why
you write so many poems about the sun?
It is

"…have patience with everything unresolved
in your heart
and try to love the questions themselves
as if they were locked rooms or books
written in a very foreign language…
Live the questions now."

Rilke

LOST 2005

Sometimes when we're lost
we discover what we would have missed
had we not been lost

I know a woman in Seattle
who couldn't find her way anywhere
unless she started from her workplace

And there's the old fellow in Ireland
who, when asked for directions, said
"Actually, you can't get there from here"

Where are the places that I'll never reach
starting from here?

VIOLIN

I knew you'd be there
in the organ gallery
lying on your side   in the scuffed-up case
I held you differently
noticed that you smell of rosin

Once you got me into trouble
after I lied about having practiced
and there you were
with two broken strings

Remember the time
the San Francisco Opera House
swallowed our sound
four young violinists
bearing down on their bows
while Gloria Parmisano banged the chimes
and the Glee Club sang "The Seraphic Song"

I used to forget you
on purpose
every Tuesday
embarrassed to carry you past those traffic boys
and had to phone my mother to bring you
like the time
I said "good-bye" and entered the convent
then phoned home for you
because we were performing on the next
Friday night

We were never very good on Czardas
But "Meditation from Thais"   Massenet's "Elegy"
                    or "Berceuse" from Jocelyn
                              we could do

I know it's my fault
          we've been playing second lately
                          I could have
                                practiced more
(but then recently you've been squawking a lot)

                    One night on TV
        I watched James Buswell III
                    play Mendelsohn's Violin Concerto
The others in the room weren't paying enough
attention
                    to see that I was crying
          Later
                    when I showed the film in Music
                                Appreciation
Maxine Noffsinger- the most unruly kid in the class-
          came up after the movie
                    and told me
                    he made her ashamed of her life

          I've always had the heart for you
                    but lacked the energy
          I wonder what you could have done
                    with someone else

COUNTERPOINT
(the art of combining melodies)

The matinee symphony
Bach and Mozart
Britten and Shostakovich
penetrating the concert hall

The Brandenburg weaving
violin, flute, oboe and trumpet
fortissimo and diminuendo
in mutual deference

Then last night "The Ground Truth"
erased the delighted faces
of the afternoon

The only applause
tears

for the destruction of a small country
with "our" oil under their ground
for creating a limitless war zone
where everyone is the enemy

children,
targets in the shooting gallery

for the damaged souls
of our own children sent overseas
with hate in their hearts
totally disoriented
believing that oil means freedom

Shouldn't this be two poems?
No, it was one day

TSUNAMI
2007

It was not yet time
So you ran from the sea
and did not stand with those
facing the wall of water
ready to return

They were mourned by survivors
but they had returned at last
"to the origin of their own origins"

Those of you who turned
back to earth
do you often reflect
on what it is
that you still have to do?

Are you trying
not to waste
this precious time
that you still have
to become you?

HOSPITAL LOBBY

2005

Automatic doors open and close
for comings and goings

Unlike other doors
a different mood
for IN and OUT

Inside this building
pain and anxiety
encounter compassion

Outside this building
if the world is falling apart
where does this lobby stand?

Here and now
the only vessel for this moment

POLLYANNA IN PAIN

The tsunami left my dreams
crossed the coastline
burying homes, families, animals
nothing there to mourn

In such a hurry
cancer invaded the womb
two eggs beginning to grow
not yet aware of their fate

Foster children unsuspecting
used as guinea pigs
doomed to death
anyway

Muslim patriots
inflamed by jihad
selling their bodies
for fuses

Mother Earth
source of life
becoming a garden
of landmines

Is anyone out there
able to play the glad game?

NEGATIVE AGES

Moving into negative ages
can cause confusion
in the pro-life and pro-choice camps

Let me explain

When I
was minus six
on 6/25/25, my atoms
were scattered around Seattle
or more accurately, around the Universe

Some of them were probably energy
with the destiny
of growing into me

So how old am I really?

You might respond
"But where
was the life?
When
did the loving relationship
come in?"

Right there
from the beginning

If there was a beginning

WEALTH 2007

Wealth cannot totally
protect us from beggars
who find ways
to invade our viewpoint

Wealth cannot totally
erase the hunger sounds
howling outside our walls

Wealth cannot totally
secure us from theft
terror, disease or death

So how could wealth ever
make us totally happy?

LIFELONG LEARNING 2006

What if
every morning
you had to remember
to give your nails
food for growing

And if
every evening
you had to research a process
for falling asleep

Wonder about this -
Your body is a university
a vast library of ancient volumes
portable and self-renewable

NEW YEAR'S EVE, 2003 2004

They came right out of me
these surprising words
"We're not made for nobility"
then to make it worse I added
"No matter what the big shots say"

My cry that neither
suffering or war is nobler
leaves the question
what to be when it appears
that what to do
is not the question

Hafiz again had the answer
"There is nothing
but Divine Movement
in this World"

So say "Whatever"

GOLDEN GLOBE AWARDS   *2005*

Lusting for affirmation
Small nuggets congregate
Attractive and glittering

Black limousines
Line up to deliver
The beautiful packages

At round tables
Expectantly they wait
For the open envelopes

The losers clap and smile
At the rising and the hugging
Of the winners

Bereft of eloquence
These highly trained voices
Stammer exhaustive thanks

The majority lose
More than an award
For performance

How in the world
Perpetually seeking roles
Can a heart find itself?

Yet, vast audiences
Attend with appreciation,
Envy and some sadness

WITHOUT TIME

can we evolve?

what do we
divide distance by
to get speed?

You see it's real
however relative

THE LEAP SECOND   *2006*

A second was indisputably defined

as one three-thousand-six-hundredth

of the twenty-fourth part of a period

of the earth's rotation on its axis.

So what's this leap second

they're sticking

into the first moment of 2006?

Oh, it's just

a wink of an eye adjustment

so we can go on believing

in absolutes.

BEANTY 2006

I
"End never justifies the means"
Remove this maxim
from the realm of philosophy
Transpose it to life's journey

When you realize this step
is equally beautiful
to being at the gates of glory
you have arrived
where the means are the end

II
It's time to refine my life
cut the crudeness
present my time
as polished moments

III
Has comfort driven beauty
from our dwellings
Has it?

Is sharpening of the sensate
the way to intensity
Is it?

Can your heart
easily reach the high notes
Can it?

Have you carefully practiced
the insignificant
Have you?

DAYLIGHT SAVINGS 2007

Who decides each year
when the flowers have not yet risen
that we lose an hour of life?

Where does it hide
til we find it in October?

Is it saved in some time bank,
security, for coping, when leaves
are falling all around us?

*"When the country falls into chaos,
patriotism is born."*

The Tao

LAST JUDGMENT

What did you spend your money on?
I spent it on war

What did you need for war?
Trucks, guns, bullets and bombs

Who started the war?
I did

Why did you start the war?
I needed oil

For what?
Cars, trucks, airplanes

Oh

MS. AMERICA

Descending the staircase
tall in a white gown
I announce
"Everyone now
will please speak English"

In my life
I have learned
to speak English
I can also sing in English

It carries
my rage and my tenderness

On trips anywhere
it travels well

I have used it
to get groceries
and to reach God

GROW UP 2007

Our founding fathers are dead.

They watch over and wonder
why we cannot let go of their hands.

They knew about leaving.
They knew about beginning,
never imagining we would
read it as ending.

They never expected us
to take their seeds
and treat them like trophies
burying this legacy
in the concrete ground
of Wall Street.

WAIT

Don't hate us
pity us
The money you envy
is our downfall

If there is
a word in Farsi
meaning downfall
use it
to deter you

CURRENT EXEGESIS

2004

"One nation
under God
indivisible
with liberty and justice
for all"

One nation
can push a button
providing death for all

Under God
perpetuates
the hierarchical myth

Indivisible
yet, simply
a part of the whole

As for liberty and justice
some have liberty
while others stalk justice

AWAKENING 2007

I'm waking up to find
I'm on the Titanic
I didn't/wouldn't listen
to all the warnings

Some say
it didn't have to happen
if they had closed the hatches
the ship was "unsinkable"

Now what to do
this unwanted awareness
of menacing water
beyond the flimsy hatches

SPECIES

Are the same folks
who couldn't care less
about their ancestors
the ones who would
never study astronomy
or paleontology
or evolutionary biology

I think they might be

They also probably park
their SUVs
on narrow suburban streets
and make regular contributions
to local land fill sites

Let's not fault them too much
It may be a genetic disorder
But let's be careful
not to elect them

IN THE BLACK 1993

Tar light slowly covers
head, shoulders and so on
Standing in this society, time
for more than greed, with
a hunger for color

Those who laugh and play
ring around the sadness
are ill, as we are
numb from news
cast black and white

Hungry for color
day brilliant
in the tended garden
where a peacock hoists
a glad flag

LIKE SEED

We call them strangers
because of food, clothes, language

They look like us
with arms, legs, eyes

They laugh and cry
like we do
and fit right in
to the working day

They too have never been
outside the atmosphere

They require air and water
return their dead to fire and earth

Like seed
borne on the wind
they come, the refugees

*"The first problem for all of us,
men and women,
is not to learn,
but to unlearn."*

Gloria Steinem

SURVIVOR 1998

Long narrow skull,
primitive thrusting jaw,
the large teeth
make her older than the Algonquins

Perforated, and strung
on a thong around her neck
a slender dagger
carved from the tine of an elk's antler
and a spiral conch

She died alone
undisturbed by friends
or wild animals
near an open forest
spruce, fir, white pine and birch,
scattered bogs of tamarack

A sudden accident
flash flood in a ravine
or a land slide
from the lake's embankment
A fifteen year old girl
embedded in layered clay
twenty thousand years
before being named
Minnesota Man

GARDEN 1983

The tree
speaks fruit
thinking
you are not directly
spoken to
thinking
you are thus inferior
thinking
the knowledge
of good and evil
is not knowledge
is thinking
is not eating

Fearing
the entrance
of the apple
fearing the knowledge
using the man
as shade
from the apple
is fearing

Why did you leave the garden?
It is his god
driving him
from the garden
Why do you go?

Among the things
which he builds
out of extra ribs
you
are near the top
Is that why you leave?
Are you climbing
the tree
instead of eating
the apple?

Why are you afraid of the apple?

HE AND SHE *2002*
Galway Kinnell and Lucille Clifton

They each spawned poems
after nine eleven
interrupted daily-ness

He described
with powerful words
insuring we never forget

She related
the aftermath
to the strangers intent

I bothered to notice
because these fine poems
stoked the stereotype

He is bleeding from the head
She from the heart

CONFLICT 1997

Denied my right to report
I resorted to malpractice,
smiling away the tridents
in your eyes.

You opened your treasure box
and showed me
your wife's softness.
You also promised
that all the corporate boards
are not meeting
at hard rectangular tables.

You then thanked me
for our conversation
and noted that our only difference
lay in implementation.

HAIR

1997

My hair
straight as a man's mind
is woven
from silken strands
into a shining braid

Only then is it pulled round
into a mandala
encircling my head
which ponders such words
as mandolin, mango
manage, maniac, manure

Until I say "Wo"
that is enough
get back to work
gather the wood
spin the wool
do something worthwhile
make yourself worthy

In my dreams, however,
I return to the wall
I punched my fist through
when first I began to be me
to flaunt the I
as in mine

The wall was stone
old and Irish
It had waited
ages for my arm

Not only did I move through
but the wall moved too
Would it have been better left
or was I right
to do the violence

Would I be less beautiful
just sitting in the sunlight
having my hair braided

WHINING 1997

I do a lot of whining
I use it every day
To help my self perception
In a clever sort of way

Responsibility is shifted
From me to everywhere
I am just the victim
Of fate or God out there

Whining's good for pressure
It releases by erosion
What could cause a lot of damage
If left to an explosion

Whining trips the switches
A safety valve in place
Each annoying plaintive whimper
Another form of grace

ANOTHER HIERARCHY   *2008*

And this time it's water
shame on you

At least you didn't
name one Lesser
and the other Least

Was it because there were five

Why slight Huron and Erie
Michigan's big enough
to take it standing
and the French one's
too arrogant to care

Besides, what's so great
about any of them

THE CONTAINER 2007

Gift of a diamond in a band-aid box
Anne-Sophie Mutter
playing Bruch's Scottish Fantasy
on a cheap transistor radio

Your pipsqueak voice
and adolescent comments
should have spoiled
your stories and poems

I found myself listening
responding to a talent
speaking in its own voice
totally authentic and sure

SHIRIN EBADI*   *2006*

Your judgeship was stolen
but no one can deprive you
of the title "Honorable"

You stand before us
and claim justice
as the characteristic
that has driven your life

This ennobles you
nurtured in repression
to preach to US
the dogmas of democracy

You do not speak
about responsibility being
the handmaiden of human rights
but your life suffices for that

Nobel Peace Laureate - 2003
Iranian lawyer and former judge
Women and Children's Rights Activist

MARY FRANCES

Wouldn't wear the required
flower in her hair.
Having no notion
why she objected
I took up her cause
with loud persuasions
around rights and freedom

Why did I think
Her Imperious Highness
needed assistance
Alone, she could have
turned back a battalion
with those dark green eyes
and flaming red hair

PARMELIA RUDECTA   *1967*

Here, take a look
　　　　at yourself
　　　　　　through my glasses.
　　Notice the flat pale green
puckering, the strong white glue
　　　　　　exuding from the walnut grip.

　　　You're lichen.

　At first I welcomed the clinging
　　　　　delicate filament
　　penetrating my surface.
　But the erosion continues
　　　　　until the core becomes the crust
until acid from the suckered bond
　　　in alternate
　wetting and drying
　　　　　consumes me.

　I am dissolving
　　　like the hardest rock
　　　or even
　　　　old window glass
　　　　becoming
　　　　　soil.

THE SCREAM

I will tell you the footnotes first.
Edvard Munch painted the scream.
Muriel Rukeyeser said the earth would break open.
Adrienne Rich dreamt of a common language.

Shelley, it's not all right
or OK as you say.
Deep down I am screaming.
A volcano is erupting
drooling lava
down the pedestal.

The musician below
and the sculptor above
beat and hammer out
their screams in the night.
When they think no one is listening
I hear them.

Men cannot scream.
They have to howl.
Their range is not high enough
to grasp the notes,
the high thin notes
amplified by terror.

A scream is intelligent.
There is a mind
that recognizes
curds of blood.
Amazement and fright
flow from comparison.

Near fear, there is anger.
Both, involve letting go
opening the throat
for an explosion -
a column
of potent energy.

The mouth, the final gate;
the last chance to muffle,
to control and conceal,
swallow the issue
and stem the gush
with a clamped smile.

The ears, cover the ears
for the sound of the scream
will batter and smash
any chords of harmony.
With a giant blow
it will crack open the earth.

Then the magma
will truly turn to lava.
Strange islands will appear
and on their beaches
will be found bodies,
those who drowned in the sound.

RADIANCE AGAINST WAR 2008

At the demonstration last evening
driving by with her friend
on the way to exercise
she came back and joined us

Using her body for a placard
waving her arms
two fingers for peace
she leaned into the street
catching driver's eyes

The honking increased
and we connected
with those whizzing by
all smiles and thumbs up

INTIMATE NATURE 1977

He was honored
when they asked him
to speak on Intimate Nature

Luckily he found
a chapter in a book
with that very title
which he unabashedly
read to us
amid personal anecdotes

Then he tried out
some guided imagery
which the polite among us
pretended worked

I think he knew
he had nothing to say
but said it anyway

MARY

1983

I am your portrait
painter.
There is a big red sigh
in the background.
Your stump
pounds on a table.
Your sharp chin
an ice pick
into my heart.
You keep flicking ashes
into my eyes
and the exorbitant scream
ticks its way into my ears
crying   help   crying.

Outside
an eagle swoops
as though
there were no
labyrinth.

FAREWELL MACHO DEI   *2004*

I knew this morning
your throne had toppled
right out of the heavens
absorbed into earth

Your laws and structures
of shriveled import

No more military salutes
for this organism

However, the full extent
is still a secret

HOWTH CASTLE 1995

Your Majesty
sitting before the cursed gate
I pictured you
ruler of seas
returned from the court
of England

Pictured you
barred from entering
Felt your fury
at this insulting
of her who commanded
formidable ships

Pictured you
standing tall
preceding your hunched people
beyond obsequity
seizing the opportunity
for retaliation

I would have laid rhododendrons
on your unknown grave
Instead I found them growing
over the Howth hills

A Tribute!
This site calls for a tribute
This sight of Ireland's Eye
and a wasted gate

MEETING 1971

"My cancer prevents me ...."
She sat in a circle of nuns
sharing ways
of implementing plans.

The possessive pronoun
stunned me.
The usual "I have cancer"
or "The cancer is spreading"
keeps it foreign.

I began to wonder
about the rooms she moved through,
trees she sat under, praying,
reading what books?
Coffee or tea, with sugar, cream?
The features of her parents?
Were her vacations
at the ocean or the mountains?
Can she remember her dreams?

I wanted
to bring her an ivory rock
put pink roses in her room,
watch her listen
to Pachelbel's Canon
instead of going on
with the meeting.

SHE SAID

She said
my Poetry Teacher
said after reading
my poems
"You make something beautiful
and then you smash it"

She was right
I've been protecting the distance
between me and the others

I've been a watchdog
guarding the border
between once and again

Waves do it too
with only one chance
to smash into beauty
against a rock

WHEVER YOU ARE, APOLOGIES
1975

to all the young women
who questioned
the reason for Algebra
and I told them
the reason
was reason was good for them

to Carla
who wanted to know when
the identity of x would be revealed

and to Sue
who resisted
in spite of a mind
that was so fine for Physics

most of all
to Mary Ellen
for laughing
when you challenged Newton
because his laws
didn't happen in your house

No,
most of all
to Patricia

The real work of religion
is permanent astonishment.

Rumi

DAWN

Dawn is not approaching
We approach dawn

We also turn away in the night
Assumed passivity is false

Nature patiently explains
our time is for action

Jesus said "Take up your cross
and follow Me."

Each of us has been granted
a lifetime of leadership

And death is not stalking us
We are stalking it

Yet, silence within
whispers "Both"

ENOUGH 2006

No longer, can we call
these ancient oak trees
ours

The days of staking claims
and building fences
are over

Even the Grand Canyon
is not large enough
to call our own

There is one home
A cloud covered
blue green globe - huge
with enough desert
bays, mountains and ocean
to sustain us all

It not only houses us
but daily feeds our blood and lungs
From it comes our skin, nails, teeth
the tears we shed
when placing our loved ones
back in its welcoming soil

Our cohabitants predate us
We have learned enough
about work from ants
and play from otters
The salmon taught us to swim
and the osprey to fly
We have nearly mastered
the spiders web
It is time for love

With growth and loveliness
Earth turns each day
so we can face light and darkness
know death and life
and carry the Divine spark
that inspires everything

"O Beauty, ever ancient, ever new
late have we loved Thee."

INCARNATION 2004

More than nine months
this infusion of divinity

What else
could have powered the explosion

and driven
this outward expansion

The living center
in infinite directions
becoming everywhere

APRIL REMINDER

Yesterday, fools day passed
Without a foolish thought
Nor a single prank

This morning
I turned the calendar
And saw a small red fox
Behind an even redder bush
Alert and so serious

Contrasting with
A smaller insert picturing
A ruby-throated hummingbird
Hovering near a fuchsia

Remember

This is Passiontide
When angels smear
The doorposts of Israel
With the blood of a lamb
And the Lamb of God is wrapped
In a scarlet military cloak
And mocked as a fool

BELOVED

2006

How do you do it
making water solid as a mirror
Any image can walk on it

I ignored your power
in favor of your beauty
Both seem to unnerve me

And where is love, the darling
I cringed at the bridal language
when we exchanged vows

It was too gushy, too familiar
for your regality
and my commonness

I wrapped my heart in a beautiful box
carefully labeled "do not open
until after death"

Yet here you are
walking on my bay toward me
with arms outstretched in every direction

In my dreams
I've always escaped the tidal waves
hurrying to safer heights

An inner well is overflowing
and all the high ground in the world
won't save me

THE SERPENT IS THE EXTRA PIECE
1965

The gates of paradise
through which we were driven
are in the mind

Everything
is here
Everything

Holy, Holy, Holy
This, This, This

To say
that to enter the naked state
we must find them
and pass through
is to make them real

SOLITUDE'S BEAUTY AND SILENCE
2008

that robin doesn't know
and cannot be told
this is a cathedral

a tiny bird paints its voice
on the landscape
and only intermittently
is hushed

forcing us to hope
for the ending
for the final note

KENMARE 2006

In pursuit of knowing
I had prepared enough facts
to impress them
that this was more than
a circle of large stones
in a field

There was the solstice connection
the buried remains
the axial stone

I spoke of ley lines
and dragon lines
which often are found
intersecting under temples

But I learned the fear from them
when they fell into silence
standing around the circle
and not entering

IT IS YOU

We're still not admitting
that it's You pounding the coasts
blowing off roofs flooding our homes

Is this love?

"Innocent people are dying"
we scream as we go on
drawing up maps and predictions

Like the Israelites in Sinai
we know how to blame leaders
to really scapegoat them

It is too awful
to let go and acknowledge
It is You.

and even more awful
to have been with You so long
and still not understand

BETWEEN THE WATERS   *1993*

Egypt deserted
drowned in pursuit

Go back
the hand-carved chariots
the steeds
Go back
this time you
can open the waters
reassemble the armies

Go on
the bitter waters
the wood soaked waters
from the twelve springs
drink

Or camp
with the water carriers

NOVEMBER PRAYER

2006

Perpetual and eternal
light and rest

Strange goal
foreign to the now
of resting in darkness
achieving in light

The dullness
of eternal rest

The frenzy
of perpetual light

Grant us
the balance

THE EXORCISM 1989

In Escher fashion
out they flew
all the unremembered memories
the fears of a lifetime
little devils
jostling each others' tails
one by one they withdrew
at the command
of one having authority
who then called for jasmine tea

FINGAL'S CAVE

Unlike Mendelssohn
without a boat
clinging to the guide wire
one cautious step after another
cursing the bifocals
step by dangerous step
on pentagonal pillars
(basalt that years before
left the Giant's Causeway)
we entered the cave where
fear became awe

Barbara brought her recorder
and we sang
Amazing Grace

MIST 2007

erased the bank
across the water
beyond it
houses, hills
the church steeple
and the shopping center
are gone
reminding us
that we cannot always see
what we know is there

OMEGA

Bay patterns follow
clouds and groping pampas.

Sunday sounds drift
between the dipping gulls.

Bristled tufts on the carmel island
sway.

Voices float
beyond the voices of the itching ants.

The wakes of ducks point
to the breath of melting ice cubes.

Shade whispers to my skin
"It will not be long."

A crane stands.

THERESE 1978

Whose life ended at its beginning
Began at its ending
Alpha dressed
in the flesh of Omega
Amen.

Printed in the United States
128186LV00002B/5/P